100 Things

you should know about

Extinction

100 Things

you should know about

Extinction

Steve Parker

Consultant: Camilla de la Bedoyere

MASON CREST PUBLISHERS INC.
370 Reed Road
Broomall, Pennsylvania 19008
(866)MCP-BOOK (toll free)
www.masoncrest.com

ISBN: 978-1-4222-1998-0
Series ISBN (15 titles): 978-1-4222-1993-5

First Printing
9 8 7 6 5 4 3 2 1

Cataloging-in-Publication Data on file with the Library of Congress.
Printed in the U.S.A.

First published in 2010 by Miles Kelly Publishing Ltd
Bardfield Centre, Great Bardfield, Essex, CM7 4SL, UK

Editorial Director: Belinda Gallagher

Art Director: Jo Brewer

Volume Designer: Andrea Slane

Junior Designer: Kayleigh Allen

Image Manager: Liberty Newton

Indexer: Eleanor Holme

Production Manager: Elizabeth Collins

Reprographics: Anthony Cambray, Stephan Davis, Ian Paulyn

ACKNOWLEDGEMENTS
The publishers would like to thank the following artists
who have contributed to this book:

Ian Jackson, Mike Foster (Maltings Partnership), Mike Saunders

Cover artwork: Ian Jackson

All other artworks are from the Miles Kelly Artwork Bank

The publishers would like to thank the following sources
for the use of their photographs:

t = top, b = bottom, l = left, r = right, c = centre

Pages 6–7 Richard Bizley/Science Photo Library; 9(c) F.H. Idzerda, (tr) South China tiger Trix1428/Dreamstime.com,
(cr) Sumatran tiger Vladimir Wrangel/Fotolia.com, (br) Malayan tiger Kitch Bain/Fotolia.com, (br) Indochinese tiger
Judy Whitton/Fotolia.com; 12(c) Paul Nevin/Photolibrary.com, (bl) clearviewstock/Fotolia.com; 13(t) Jonathan Blair/Corbis,
(br) Stouffer Productions/Photolibrary.com; 15(cl) RGBKew, (br) Corbis; 16 Gerard Lacz/FLPA; 17(c) Fotolia.com,
(br) John Glover/Alamy; 18 Mary Evans Picture Library/Alamy; 19 Icon/Everett/Rex Features; 28(t) Artmedia/HIP/TopFoto,
(b) National Geographic/Getty Images; 29 Howard Rice/Photolibrary.com; 30–31 Eric Baccega/Naturepl.com;
31(b) Bruce Beehler/NHPA; 32(c) Photoinjection/Dreamstime.com, (b) The Granger Collection/TopFoto; 33(t) The Granger
Collection/TopFoto, (b) Topham Picturepoint/Topfoto; 36(t) sisu/Fotolia.com; 37(t) Alex Hofford/Corbis,
(b) Patricia Fogden/Corbis; 39(t) NHPA/Photoshot, (c) Jefery/Fotolia.com, (b) Naluphoto/Dreamstime.com;
40 Andrew Harrington/Naturepl.com; 41(c) Picture Press/Alamy, (b) Martin Harvey/Corbis;
42–43 Purestock/Photolibrary.com 44(t) Photos 12/Alamy, (b) Simon Littlejohn/Minden Pictures/FLPA;
45(t) AFP/Getty Images, (b) Philippe Psaila/Science Photo Library

All other photographs are from:

Corel, digitalSTOCK, digitalvision, ImageState, PhotoDisc

Contents

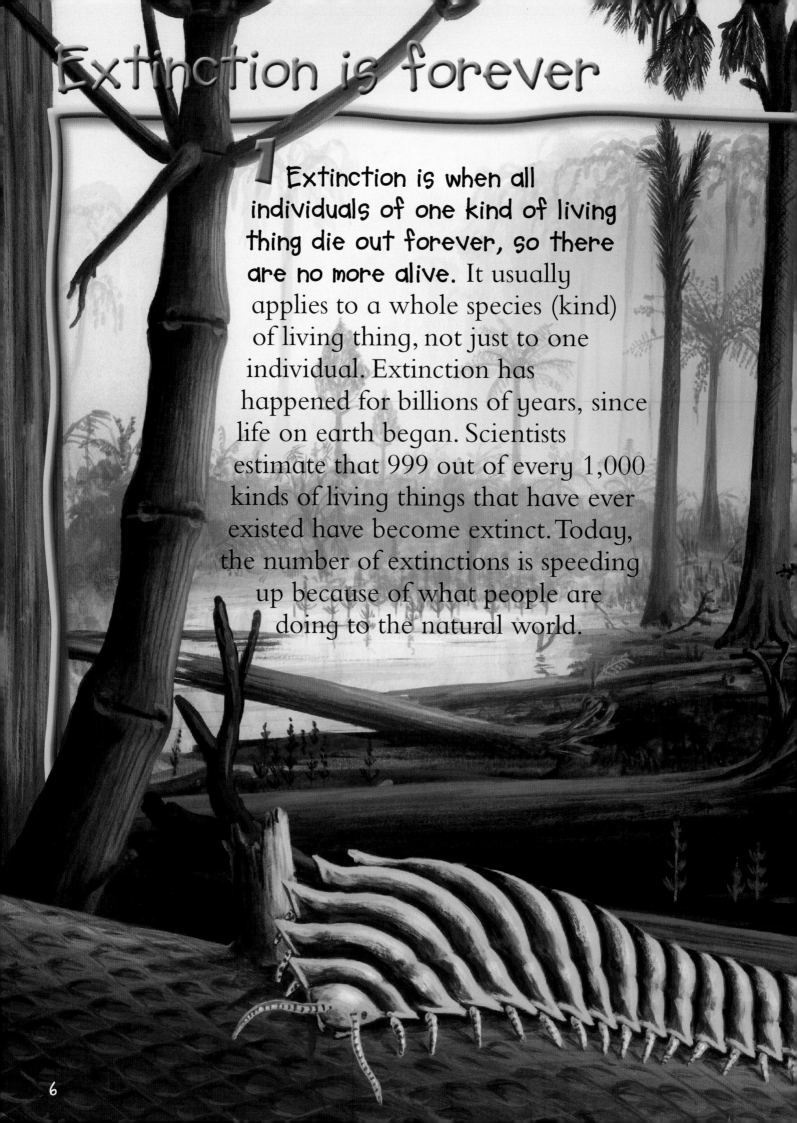

Extinction is forever

1 Extinction is when all individuals of one kind of living thing die out forever, so there are no more alive. It usually applies to a whole species (kind) of living thing, not just to one individual. Extinction has happened for billions of years, since life on earth began. Scientists estimate that 999 out of every 1,000 kinds of living things that have ever existed have become extinct. Today, the number of extinctions is speeding up because of what people are doing to the natural world.

▼ Giant dragonflies, millipedes as big as dining tables and enormous tree ferns once inhabited forests 300 million years ago. However, all of the creatures in this prehistoric swamp have long been extinct.

What is extinction?

2 Extinction is the dying out of a particular kind, or type, of living thing. It is gone forever and can never come back (although this may change in the future, see page 44). Extinction affects plants such as flowers and trees, as well as fungi such as mushrooms and molds. It also affects tiny worms and bugs, and big creatures such as dinosaurs and mammoths.

▲ The "terror bird" *Phorusrhacos* lived ten million years ago. Nothing like it survives today.

▲ There were hundreds of kinds of sea scorpions (eurypterids) 250 million years ago, but all died out.

3 Extinction is linked to how we classify (group) living things. It usually applies to a species. A species includes all living things that look similar and breed to produce more of their kind. For instance, all lions belong to one species, which scientists call *Panthera leo*.

4 One example of an extinct species is the giant elk *Megaloceros giganteus* of the last Ice Age. The last ones died out almost 8,000 years ago. But not all elk species became extinct. A similar but separate species, the elk (moose) *Alces alces*, is still alive today.

◀ Hunting by Stone Age people may have played a part in the giant elk's disappearance.

QUIZ

Which of these could, perhaps, one day become extinct?
1. Great white sharks 2. Robots
3. Daisies 4. Cameras with rolls of film (not digital)
5. Satellites 6. Houseflies

Answers:
Only living things can become extinct, so the answers are 1, 3 and 6

5 Sometimes extinction affects a subspecies. This is a group of animals within a species, that are all very similar to each other, and slightly different from others in the species. All tigers today belong to one species, *Panthera tigris*. There were once eight subspecies of tiger. Two have become extinct in the past 100 years, the Balinese tiger and the Javan tiger.

▶ All six living subspecies of tiger differ slightly—and all are threatened with extinction.

Bengal tiger

South China tiger

Siberian tiger

Sumatran tiger

Malayan tiger

Indochinese tiger

▲ The last Balinese tiger, the smallest subspecies, was killed in 1937.

6 Extinction can also affect a group of closely related species, which is called a genus. There have been about ten species of mammoths over the last two million years. They all belonged to the genus *Mammuthus*, including the wooly mammoth and the steppe mammoth. All mammoths have died out, so the genus is extinct.

◀ The Columbian mammoth, one of the biggest in the genus, died out by 12,000 years ago.

Extinction and evolution

7 Extinctions have happened through billions of years of prehistory as a natural part of evolution. Evolution is the gradual change in living things, resulting in new species appearing. As this happened, other species could not survive and became extinct.

◀ Today's hagfish differ little from their extinct cousins millions of years ago, but they are a separate species.

8 Evolution occurs as the result of changing conditions. Living things adapt to become better suited to conditions as they change, such as the weather and types of habitats (living places).

▶ Unlike the hagfish, the extinct armored fish *Hemicyclaspis* from 400 million years ago has no living relatives.

I DON'T BELIEVE IT!

Trilobites were a group of marine creatures that survived for almost 300 million years. Within that time at least 18,000 kinds came and went. The last trilobites died out in a mass extinction 250 million years ago.

Angelina
490 million years ago

Trinucleus
450 million years ago

Kolihapeltis
400 million years ago

▲ Many different kinds of trilobites evolved and died out over millions of years.

9 Scientists know about long-gone extinct species from their fossils. These are remains of body parts such as the bones, teeth, horns, claws and shells of animals, and the bark, roots and leaves of plants, which have been preserved in rocks and turned to stone.

► *Stegosaurus* was one of the longest-lasting dinosaur species. Its kind survived for over ten million years.

▼ Magnolias are flowering plants that have successfully evolved from 100 million years ago to today.

10 Studying millions of fossils of thousands of extinct species all around the world shows how different kinds of living things came and went long ago. This "turnover" of species gives the average rate of extinction. For every one million species, one species would die out about once each year.

▲ Scientists have studied more than one million trilobite fossils.

11 Fossil studies show the typical time for a species or genus to survive before going extinct. A mammal species lasted from one to two million years. For sea-living invertebrates (creatures without backbones) such as crabs, species survived between five and ten million years.

Why does it happen?

12 There are several reasons for extinction. Many extinctions are combinations of these reasons. We cannot know for sure why prehistoric species became extinct. But we can see the reasons for extinctions today. These may help us to understand what happened in the past.

13 One reason for extinction is competition. A species cannot meet enough of its needs, for food or living space, because other species need them too, and are better at getting them. These competing species may be newly evolved, or may have spread from afar.

14 A species can be forced to extinction by predators, parasites or diseases. Again, all of these could be new dangers as a result of evolution.

▼ In Australia, introduced farm animals such as sheep, and also wild rabbits, have been better than local species at gaining food.

▲ Australia's rock wallabies have suffered due to competition from sheep and goats.

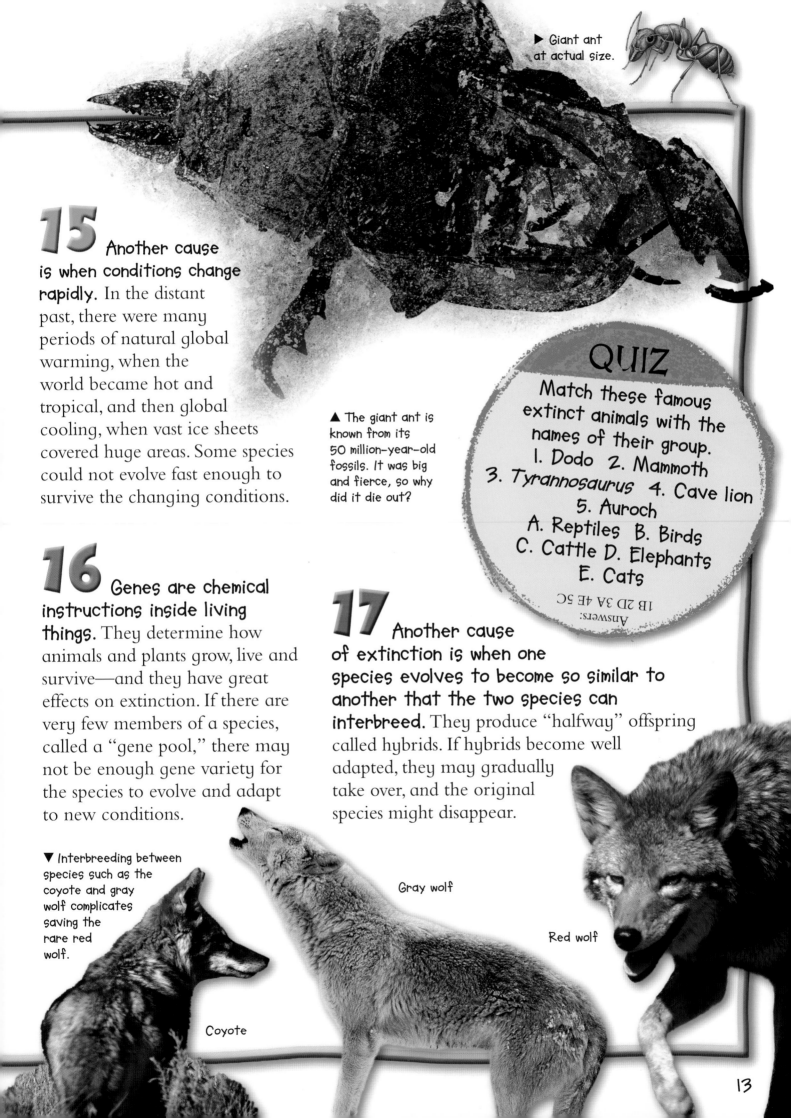

▶ Giant ant at actual size.

15 Another cause is when conditions change rapidly. In the distant past, there were many periods of natural global warming, when the world became hot and tropical, and then global cooling, when vast ice sheets covered huge areas. Some species could not evolve fast enough to survive the changing conditions.

▲ The giant ant is known from its 50 million-year-old fossils. It was big and fierce, so why did it die out?

QUIZ

Match these famous extinct animals with the names of their group.
1. Dodo 2. Mammoth
3. Tyrannosaurus 4. Cave lion
5. Auroch
A. Reptiles B. Birds
C. Cattle D. Elephants
E. Cats

Answers:
1B 2D 3A 4E 5C

16 Genes are chemical instructions inside living things. They determine how animals and plants grow, live and survive—and they have great effects on extinction. If there are very few members of a species, called a "gene pool," there may not be enough gene variety for the species to evolve and adapt to new conditions.

17 Another cause of extinction is when one species evolves to become so similar to another that the two species can interbreed. They produce "halfway" offspring called hybrids. If hybrids become well adapted, they may gradually take over, and the original species might disappear.

▼ Interbreeding between species such as the coyote and gray wolf complicates saving the rare red wolf.

Gray wolf

Red wolf

Coyote

How do we know?

18 **How do we know if a species is extinct?** The more recent the extinction, the harder it is to say. How long should we wait before saying a species is extinct? It might be found living in a remote area years later.

19 **Wildlife experts at the IUCN** (International Union for Conservation of Nature) say that a species cannot be declared extinct until 50 years have passed with no real sightings of it, or evidence such as droppings or eggshells.

▲ Leadbeater's possums were restricted to a very small area, as land around was turned into farms.

20 **Sometimes, a species thought to be extinct "comes back from the dead."** Usually it has survived in an unexplored area. It is called a "Lazarus species" after a man in the Bible who came to life again after he died.

21 **One "Lazarus species" is the squirrel-like Leadbeater's possum of Australia.** It was thought to be extinct by the 1930s, but in 1965, a group was found living in highland forests in Southeast Australia. Plant "Lazarus species" include the jellyfish tree and Monte Diablo buckwheat.

22 Some people consider creatures such as the yeti (abominable snowman), bunyip and Bigfoot to be extinct. But most scientists would say that these creatures are only from tales and legends. There is no real scientific proof they ever lived, so they cannot be extinct.

23 Some species are "extinct in the wild." This means all surviving members are in zoos, wildlife parks or gardens. One example is the toromiro, a tree that disappeared from Easter Island in the Pacific. Experts saved some at Kew Gardens, London, and it is now being taken back to its original home.

▶ A toromiro flower. The toromiro tree once covered parts of Easter Island, but it was wiped out in the wild.

▲ The huge, hairy yeti of the Himalayas is well known in myths and stories, but no real evidence of its existance has been discovered.

▼ In 1987, only 22 Californian condors were left in the wild. All were captured for breeding and chicks were raised using "condor parent" puppet gloves.

FAME AT LAST

You will need:
books about Australia
the Internet

Look in books or on the Internet for information about the state of Victoria in Australia. See if you can find the state's animal emblem or symbol, and a picture of it. That's Leadbeater's possum!

Not quite extinct

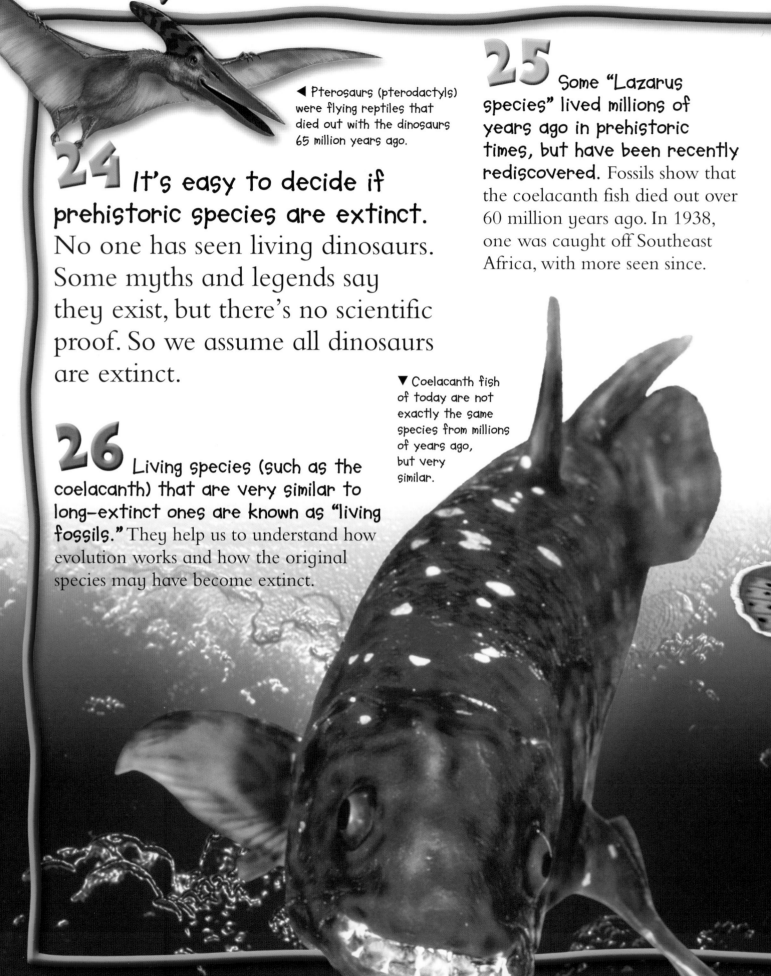

◀ Pterosaurs (pterodactyls) were flying reptiles that died out with the dinosaurs 65 million years ago.

24 It's easy to decide if prehistoric species are extinct. No one has seen living dinosaurs. Some myths and legends say they exist, but there's no scientific proof. So we assume all dinosaurs are extinct.

25 Some "Lazarus species" lived millions of years ago in prehistoric times, but have been recently rediscovered. Fossils show that the coelacanth fish died out over 60 million years ago. In 1938, one was caught off Southeast Africa, with more seen since.

26 Living species (such as the coelacanth) that are very similar to long-extinct ones are known as "living fossils." They help us to understand how evolution works and how the original species may have become extinct.

▼ Coelacanth fish of today are not exactly the same species from millions of years ago, but very similar.

27 When a particular species is known to be living, it is called "extant" rather than "extinct." Other examples of extant "living fossils" include Australia's Wollemi pine tree, the pig-like Chacoan peccary, and the shellfish known as the lampshell.

▲ The Chacoan peccary is similar to the giant Ice Age peccary that disappeared 10,000 years ago.

28 A tree "living fossil" once thought to be extinct is the dawn redwood. It was known only from fossils dating back ten million years. Then in 1944, examples were found in China. The living species, *Metasequoia glyptostroboides*, is slightly different to the long-extinct species.

◀ The dawn redwood, one of only three redwood species, is now planted in parks and gardens across the world.

◀ Large copper butterflies are still found in mainland Europe, but habitats lost to farming mean they are rare.

29 A particular plant or creature may become extinct in one area but be extant in another. In Europe, the large copper butterfly became extinct in Britain in the 1860s, but it still lives in many other places across the region.

Beliefs and ideas

30 **The way people view extinction has changed through the ages.** Scientists' thoughts can be very different to those of other people. Some people don't believe in extinction, perhaps due to religious ideas.

31 **In ancient times, people such as the Greek scientist-naturalist Aristotle (384–322 BCE) believed that the natural world had never changed.** No new species evolved and no old ones became extinct.

32 **As people began to study fossils, they realized that they were from living things that were no longer around.** Some experts said these plants and animals survived somewhere remote and undiscovered. Others began to suggest that extinction really did happen.

33 **Fossil expert Georges Cuvier (1769–1832) was one of the first scientists to say that there probably were extinctions.** Due to his religious beliefs, he explained them as happening in the Great Floods described in the Bible.

▼ Baron Georges Cuvier admitted that the fossil elephants he studied had become extinct.

GOOD AND BAD EXTINCTIONS

Make a list of animals that can cause problems such as spreading diseases, eating farmers' crops and damaging trees. Ask your family and friends: If you could make some extinct, which ones would you choose and why? Does everyone have the same answers? Here's a few to get you started: Houseflies, fleas, rats, squirrels, pigeons, foxes, deer.

▲ By altering the malaria-carrying mosquito's genes, scientists may be able to wipe out the disease malaria.

▼ In South America, Darwin studied fossils of the giant armadillo-like *Glyptodon* and wondered why it no longer survived.

35 **Modern views continue to change about extinction.** Scientists can now identify separate species by studying their genes, rather than what they look like or how they breed. What was thought to be one species could, with genetic information, be two or more. For endangered plants and animals, it might not be one species threatened with extinction, but several.

34 **In 1859, extinction became an important topic.** Naturalist Charles Darwin described the theory of evolution in his book *On the Origin of Species by Means of Natural Selection*. In it Darwin explained the idea of "survival of the fittest," and how new species evolved while other species less equipped to deal with their environment died out.

▶ A scene from the 2009 movie *Creation*. Darwin's ideas about evolution shaped modern scientific views on extinction.

Long, long ago

36 The history of life on Earth dates back over three billion years, and extinction has been happening since then. Millions of plants and animals have died out over this time, called the geological timescale.

37 Fossil evidence shows that even 500 million years ago, there was an enormous variety of life, with many species becoming extinct. The idea that long ago there were just a few species, which gradually increased through to today, with new ones evolving but very few dying out, is not accurate.

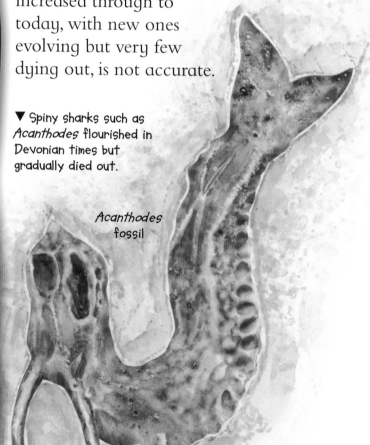

▼ Spiny sharks such as *Acanthodes* flourished in Devonian times but gradually died out.

Acanthodes fossil

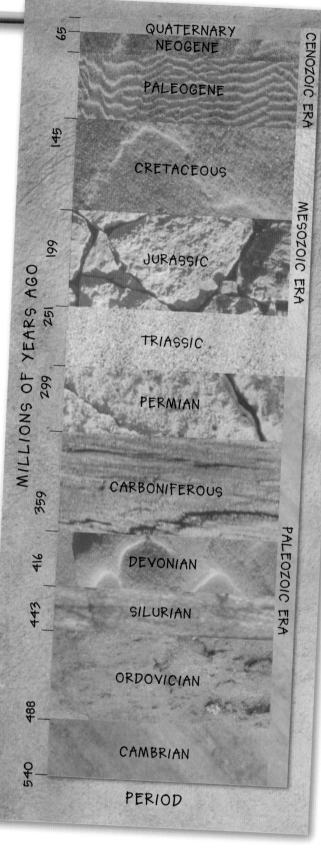

MILLIONS OF YEARS AGO

65	QUATERNARY / NEOGENE
	PALEOGENE
145	CRETACEOUS
199	JURASSIC
251	TRIASSIC
299	PERMIAN
359	CARBONIFEROUS
416	DEVONIAN
443	SILURIAN
488	ORDOVICIAN
540	CAMBRIAN

CENOZOIC ERA
MESOZOIC ERA
PALEOZOIC ERA

PERIOD

▲ The geological timescale spans the history of the Earth. This vast amount of time is broken down into eras, and then into time periods. By studying fossils from different periods we can see how abundant life was through prehistory.

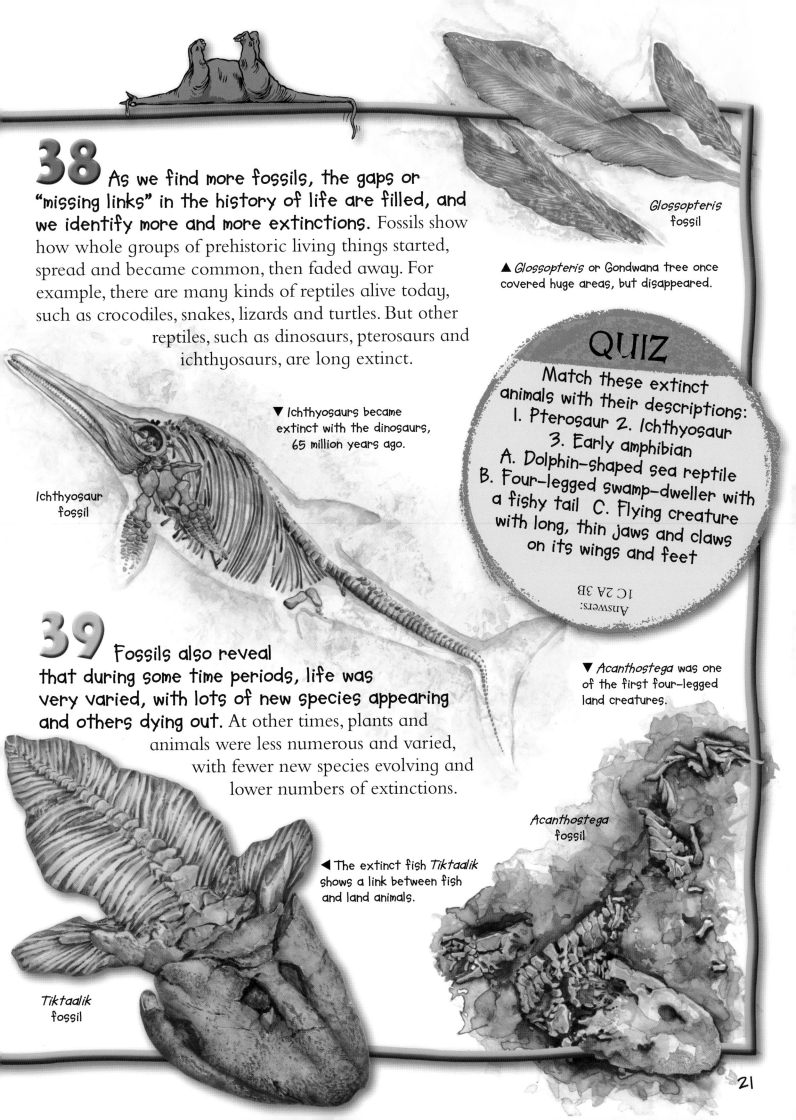

38 As we find more fossils, the gaps or "missing links" in the history of life are filled, and we identify more and more extinctions. Fossils show how whole groups of prehistoric living things started, spread and became common, then faded away. For example, there are many kinds of reptiles alive today, such as crocodiles, snakes, lizards and turtles. But other reptiles, such as dinosaurs, pterosaurs and ichthyosaurs, are long extinct.

Glossopteris fossil

▲ *Glossopteris* or Gondwana tree once covered huge areas, but disappeared.

▼ Ichthyosaurs became extinct with the dinosaurs, 65 million years ago.

Ichthyosaur fossil

QUIZ

Match these extinct animals with their descriptions:
1. Pterosaur 2. Ichthyosaur 3. Early amphibian
A. Dolphin-shaped sea reptile
B. Four-legged swamp-dweller with a fishy tail C. Flying creature with long, thin jaws and claws on its wings and feet

Answers:
1C 2A 3B

39 Fossils also reveal that during some time periods, life was very varied, with lots of new species appearing and others dying out. At other times, plants and animals were less numerous and varied, with fewer new species evolving and lower numbers of extinctions.

▼ *Acanthostega* was one of the first four-legged land creatures.

Acanthostega fossil

◄ The extinct fish *Tiktaalik* shows a link between fish and land animals.

Tiktaalik fossil

Mass extinctions

40 At times in the Earth's history there have been mass extinctions, also called extinction events. Huge numbers of living things died out in a short time, usually less than a few thousand years. In some cases, over half of all animals and plants disappeared. The main causes of mass extinctions are described on page 24.

▶ These are just a few of the millions of animals and plants that died out during mass extinctions.

41 The Cambrian-Ordovician mass extinction was 488 million years ago. It marked the change from the time span called the Cambrian Period to the next one, the Ordovician Period. Among the victims were many kinds of trilobites and lampshells, a kind of shellfish.

▶ Mass extinctions show as dips in the variety of living things throughout prehistoric time.

ORDOVICIAN-SILURIAN
450-443 million years ago

Endoceras:
A type of mollusc

CAMBRIAN-ORDOVICIAN
488 million years ago

Pikaia:
An eel-like creature with a rod-like spinal column

42 The Ordovician-Silurian mass extinction happened 450-443 million years ago, in two bursts. All life was in the sea at that time. Many types of shellfish, echinoderms (starfish, sea urchins and relatives) and corals died out.

Cambrian-Ordovician

Ordovician-Silurian

600   500   400   Time (million years ago)

Triceratops:
One of the last
dinosaurs

43 **The Late Devonian mass extinction included several bursts 365–359 million years ago.** Corals, trilobites and several groups of fish disappeared. It was the end of the "Age of Fishes."

LATE DEVONIAN
365–359 million years ago

TRIASSIC-JURASSIC
200 million years ago

Placodus:
A marine
reptile

Dunkleosteus:
An armored fish

44 **The Triassic-Jurassic mass extinction occurred 200 million years ago.** The main groups affected included many sea creatures, amphibians, and certain types of reptiles, including some early dinosaurs.

45 **The Cretaceous-Tertiary mass extinction, 65 million years ago, is the most famous.** It saw the extinction of the dinosaurs, as well as many other animals and plants. More than two-thirds of all species died out. The cause may have been a meteorite that smashed into Earth, setting off earthquakes, tsunamis and volcanoes, and causing rapid climate change.

800

Number of families

Late Devonian

Triassic-Jurassic

Cretaceous-Tertiary

0

200

100

0

23

The biggest of all

46 The most massive of all mass extinctions was the Permian–Triassic or end-of-Permian event, 251 million years ago. Also known as the "Great Dying," it saw vast losses, with more than four-fifths of all Earth's species wiped out.

47 The "Great Dying" was probably caused by the same combination of reasons as several other mass extinctions. These included volcanic eruptions, earthquakes and tsunamis. They were probably set off by the continents drifting into new positions, with accompanying changes in sea levels, ocean currents, wind patterns, rainfall and temperature.

▶ At the end of the Permian Period, the world was rocked by a series of great changes that killed off most kinds of life on Earth.

48 The changes that probably caused mass extinctions were very complicated because of the way species depend on each other. If a particular plant could not cope with the changes and died out, then the animals that fed on it were also affected, as were the predators that fed on them. The balance of nature was upset and extinctions followed.

Acanthodian fish

Crinoids

Placoderms

49 Mass extinctions upset some habitats more than others. In many of these events, including the Permian-Triassic one, most losses were marine life. Especially affected were tiny sea plants and creatures that formed the floating "soup" of life known as plankton.

Diictodon

Lystrosaurus

Gorgonops

Corals

Trilobites

50 Mass extinctions were not total disasters. Afterward, fewer species meant less competition. So there were chances and opportunities for a surge of evolution and new species. Just 20 million years after the Permian-Triassic "Great Dying," the first dinosaurs were prowling the land while early pterosaurs flapped through the skies.

51 Over the past few million years, there have been several extinctions linked to more than a dozen ice ages. The first of these started around 2.6 million years ago, and the last one faded just 15,000–10,000 years ago. These cold times are called glaciations, and the warmer periods between—like the one today—are interglacials.

52 An example of an extinct ice age species is the saber-tooth cat *Smilodon*. There were perhaps five species of *Smilodon* starting around 2.5 million years ago. The last one, dying out only 10,000 years ago, was *Smilodon fatalis*.

▲ Last of the ice age saber-tooth cats, *Smilodon* lived in the Americas and was as big as the largest big cat of today, the Siberian tiger.

53 Hundreds of other ice age animals have died out in the past 25,000 years. They include the wooly rhino, wooly mammoth, cave bear, dire wolf, and various kinds of horses, deer, camels, llamas, beavers, ground sloths, and even mice and rats.

54 Many of these large animals disappeared during a fairly short time period of 15,000– 10,000 years ago. This happened especially across northern lands in North America, Europe and Asia. What was the cause of such widespread losses?

55 Two main reasons have been suggested for the recent ice age extinctions. One is rapid natural climate change. As the weather warmed up, some big animals could not evolve fast enough or travel to cooler areas. The wooly mammoth and wooly rhino, for example, may have overheated.

56 The second reason is the spread of humans. As the climate warmed, ice sheets and glaciers melted, and people moved north into new areas. Big animals such as mammoths were hunted for food, as shown in Stone Age cave paintings. Others, such as cave bears, were killed because they were dangerous.

▼ Low sea levels during ice ages allowed people to spread from Eastern Asia to North America.

SIBERIA

ARCTIC OCEAN

NORTH AMERICA

Alaska

PACIFIC OCEAN

▶ Stone Age people probably trapped and killed mammoths, which would have provided them with food for weeks.

Keeping a record

57 In ancient times, people traveled little and did not record details of nature, so extinctions were hard to identify. From the 1500s on, people began to explore the world, study living things and discover new species. They then hunted, shot, ate or collected them—some to extinction.

▲ People exploring remote areas brought back tales of fanciful beasts—perhaps the result of several real creatures that explorers mixed up.

58 Spectacular examples of historical extinction are the elephant birds of Madagascar. There were several species of these giant, flightless birds, similar to ostriches but larger. The biggest stood 10 feet (3 meters) tall and weighed more than 1,000 pounds (about 450 kilograms).

59 All elephant birds were extinct by the 1500s. People not only hunted them, but also collected and cooked their huge eggs, more than 14 inches (35 centimeters) in length.

▼ Elephant birds evolved on the island of Madagascar with no big predators to threaten them—until humans arrived.

Steller's sea cow was 26 feet (8 meters) long

Bluebuck lived in small herds

Great auks once numbered millions

▲ Extinctions of large creatures continued through recent centuries.

60 There is a long list of other animal species that went extinct even before 1900. They include the tall New Zealand ground birds called moas (by 1500), the huge European cow known as the auroch (probably 1630s), the North Pacific Steller's sea cow (1760s), the Southern African bluebuck antelope (around 1800) and the Atlantic penguin-like great auk (1850s).

61 Many plants are also recorded as going extinct during this time. They include the Rio myrtle tree from South America (about 1820s), the string tree from the Atlantic island of St. Helena (1860s) and the Indian kerala tree (1880s).

◀ St. Helena ebony is a shrub that is being rescued from the brink of extinction.

Gathering pace

62 Over the last 100 years, the rate of extinction has speeded up greatly. More kinds of living things are disappearing than ever before. This is due mainly to human activity such as cutting down forests, habitat loss as natural areas are changed for farmland and houses, hunting, collecting rare species, and releasing chemicals into the environment.

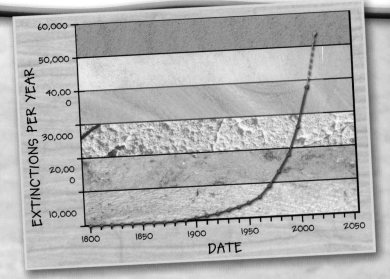

▲ The estimated extinction rate is rocketing as we find out about more threatened species every year.

▶ The spectacled bear of South America's Andes Mountains faces many threats, including the logging of its forest home.

63 One of the first extinctions to receive lots of publicity around the world was the Caribbean monk seal in the 1950s. It was hunted for its oil and meat, and to stop it eating the fish that people wanted to catch. From 2003, expeditions tried to find it again but gave up after five years.

▲ The last confirmed sightings of Caribbean monk seals were southeast of the island of Jamaica in 1952.

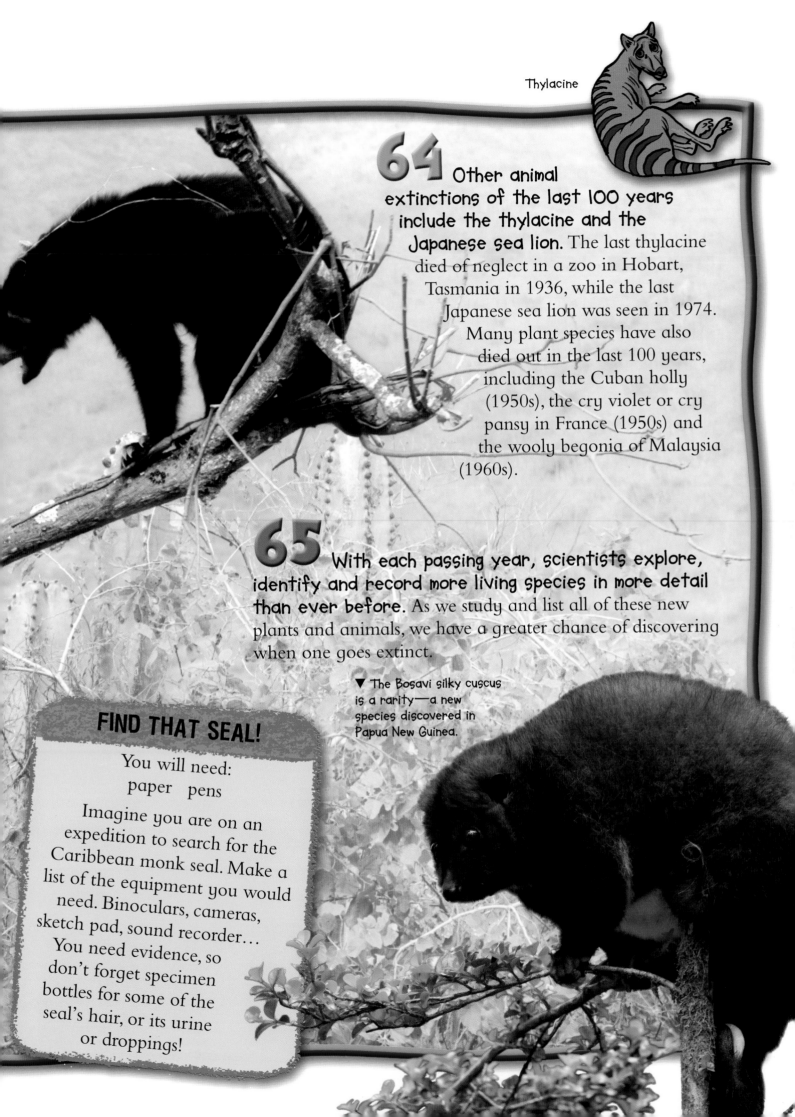

Thylacine

64 Other animal extinctions of the last 100 years include the thylacine and the Japanese sea lion. The last thylacine died of neglect in a zoo in Hobart, Tasmania in 1936, while the last Japanese sea lion was seen in 1974. Many plant species have also died out in the last 100 years, including the Cuban holly (1950s), the cry violet or cry pansy in France (1950s) and the wooly begonia of Malaysia (1960s).

65 With each passing year, scientists explore, identify and record more living species in more detail than ever before. As we study and list all of these new plants and animals, we have a greater chance of discovering when one goes extinct.

▼ The Bosavi silky cuscus is a rarity—a new species discovered in Papua New Guinea.

FIND THAT SEAL!

You will need:
paper   pens

Imagine you are on an expedition to search for the Caribbean monk seal. Make a list of the equipment you would need. Binoculars, cameras, sketch pad, sound recorder… You need evidence, so don't forget specimen bottles for some of the seal's hair, or its urine or droppings!

Too many to disappear

66 The passenger pigeon was once extremely common. Flocks of millions flew around North America, darkening the skies as they passed. Before Europeans arrived in North America, native people caught the pigeons for their meat and feathers. This was on a small scale and happened for centuries without affecting the overall number of birds.

67 With the arrival of Europeans, especially from about 1700, came many changes. The new settlers altered the land from natural habitats to farms, roads and towns. Habitat loss soon gathered pace, and people also began to catch the pigeons for a cheap supply of food.

▼ Today, birds such as these city starlings seem too numerous to vanish. But we cannot be sure how they will fare in the future.

► Passenger pigeons became big business, with hunters shooting and trappers netting the birds to sell their meat in cities.

▲ Famous hunter, naturalist and artist John James Audobon painted passenger pigeons. He once said one flock was "still passing in undiminished numbers... for three days."

68 By the 1850s, the hunters and trappers noticed that passenger pigeon numbers had started to fall. But the killing continued. Some people tried to raise the pigeons in captivity, but the birds could only breed and thrive in very large flocks. Kept in small groups, they did not eat well or breed. They may have also suffered from a bird illness called Newcastle disease.

69 By 1900, the passenger pigeon had just about disappeared in the wild. The last one in captivity, Martha, died in Cincinnati Zoo, Ohio, in 1914. With her went one of the most numerous birds that ever existed.

I DON'T BELIEVE IT!

Martha, the last passenger pigeon, was named after Martha Washington, wife of the first U.S. president George Washington. There are several statues and memorials to Martha (the pigeon), including one at the Cincinnati Zoo.

▲ Passenger pigeons did not survive well in captivity. When the last one died in 1914, it was mounted, or "stuffed," at the Smithsonian Institute.

Island extinctions

Hawaii

CUBA

▼ Tiny islands in vast oceans around the world are "hotbeds" of extinctions.

Galapagos Islands

Cuban solenodon—this shrew-like creature has not been seen since 1999

Hawaiian black mamo —gone by the 1920s

PACIFIC OCEAN

Galapagos damselfish —became extinct during the 1980s

SOUTHERN ATLANTIC OCEAN

70 In the past few centuries, more than two-thirds of living things becoming extinct have lived on islands. Islands can support only small numbers of a particular species, so there is a higher risk of dying out. Each island also has its own particular conditions, to which species adapt over thousands of years. If conditions change, for example, when people arrive, the local wild species may be threatened.

71 Island plants and animals are also at great risk from introduced species—those brought by people. These introduced species include sheep, goats, cows, foxes, stoats, mice, rats, cats and dogs. They start to compete with the local species for food, or prey on them, or steal their nest sites, or give them diseases—or all of these.

PACIFIC OCEAN

MAURITIUS

Lesser bilby—not seen on the island continent of Australia since the 1950s

AUSTRALIA

INDIAN OCEAN

Mauritius dodo —disappeared by the 1690s

THE DODO LIVES AGAIN!

You will need:
sheet of cardboard   scissors
colored pens   sticky tape   elastic

Cut out a face mask in the shape of a dodo's head and beak and color it as shown (left). Find out from books or the Internet about the noises a dodo made. Now you can try to bring the dodo back to life!

72 Perhaps the most famous example of any extinct animal is the dodo. This flightless, turkey-sized bird lived on Mauritius in the Indian Ocean, ate fruit and nested on the ground. It had no natural predators or enemies. Then people arrived with animals that hunted it, its eggs and its chicks. By 1700, the dodo was gone, leading to the saying "dead as a dodo."

73 At least 50 bird species from the Hawaiian Islands are extinct. This affected other wildlife. Some of the birds fed on nectar and carried pollen so that flowers could breed. Others ate fruits and spread the seeds in their droppings. Without the birds, some of these plants become extinct. When one species disappears, then another that depends on it dies out, it is known as co-extinction.

What's happening today?

74 In the natural world today, extinction rates are shooting up due to a huge variety of causes. Scientists call this another time of mass extinction.

75 The main cause of today's extinctions is habitat loss and degradation (changing natural habitats for the worse). The number of people in the world is rising fast and they need land for their houses, farms, factories, roads and leisure, leaving less wild areas.

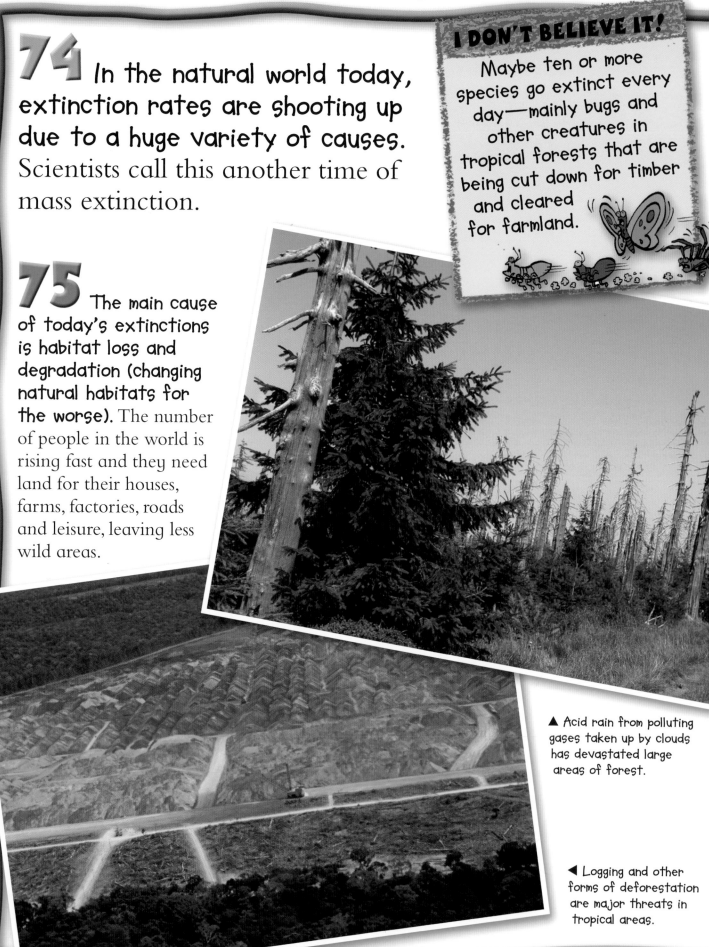

▲ Acid rain from polluting gases taken up by clouds has devastated large areas of forest.

◄ Logging and other forms of deforestation are major threats in tropical areas.

76 Other causes include pollution and hunting for food or trophies. There is also the collecting of species for displays, introduced species, and diseases that spread from domestic animals and farm plants to wild species. As the early signs of global warming and climate change become more marked, these will also have huge effects on habitats and push species toward extinction.

▲ The baiji is probably now extinct. Some people hope it survives in backwaters of the Yangtze and nearby rivers. There are rare sightings, but for the time being, no proof.

77 In 2007, a search in China failed to find any baijis, or Yangtze river dolphins. This species was threatened for many reasons, including dams built across its rivers, pollution, hunting and the overfishing of its natural prey.

▼ Now extinct, golden toads were probably victims of global warming and increased human activity in their natural habitats.

On the brink

78 Every year, wildlife experts make lists of animals and plants that are threatened with extinction. These are known as the IUCN "Red Lists," and every year, they grow longer.

► Symbols indicate if a species is threatened or not, ranging from LC meaning Least Concern, to EX meaning Extinct.

QUIZ

Which of these amphibians is threatened with extinction?
1. Lungless Mexican salamander
2. South African ghost frog
3. Betic midwife toad
4. Chinese giant salamander
5. Darwin frog

Answer:
All of them, plus thousands of others

79 One of the most endangered groups of animals is the rhinos. There are only five rhino species and all are in huge trouble. The black, Javan and Sumatran rhinos are listed as "critically endangered." They will become extinct in 20–50 years unless massive efforts are made to save them.

▼ All rhinos need action to save them. Most numerous is the white rhino, with less than 20,000.

White rhino

Sumatran rhino

Javan rhino

Black rhino

80
A larger group, with many species at risk of extinction, is the amphibians. More than half of the 6,000-plus species are threatened. A terrible problem is the new fungus infection called chytrid disease. Recent amphibian extinctions include the gastric-brooding frog of Australia, which swallowed its eggs so the tadpoles could grow in its stomach. It died out in the 1980s.

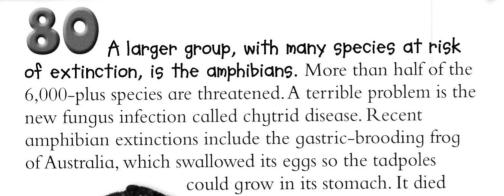

▲ Baby gastric-brooding frogs emerged from their mother's mouth. Many other species of frogs, toads and newts are also under threat.

▲ The world's largest flower, rafflesia, is now extremely rare.

81
You cannot get closer to extinction than only one remaining individual. The café marron bush grew on the island of Rodrigues in the Indian Ocean, but finally only one bush was left. Scientists at Kew Gardens, London took cuttings from it in the 1980s and grew them into bushes. Now some are being taken back to Rodrigues.

Indian rhino

82
Coral reefs are among the world's richest places for wildlife. But these whole habitats may become extinct in the next 100–200 years. They are in great danger from threats such as global warming, pollution, water cloudiness and acidity upsetting the delicate natural balance between their species.

▶ Due to global warming, coral reefs may become "bleached" and die.

Saved just in time

83 To save an almost extinct species takes time, effort and money. This means studying it and its habitat, its contact with other species and finding out how many are left. Scientists assess its needs through field studies—in the wild—and also captive studies. They establish what it eats, where it nests or which soil it likes, so that places can be put aside.

Female

Male

▲ Through a huge conservation effort, the numbers of ladybird spiders in Great Britain have risen.

84 Rescuing a threatened animal or plant from extinction also means saving its habitat. Without somewhere natural and safe to live, the species cannot thrive in the wild. Otherwise, even if it is saved, it will always be limited to a park, zoo or similar place, and be extinct in the wild.

▼ In North America, movements of very rare black-footed ferrets are studied by radio transmitter collars.

SAVE OUR SPIDER

You will need:
large sheet of paper
colored pens

Spiders may not be everyone's favorite animal, but they deserve saving as much as other species. Find out about the ladybird spider, which is almost extinct in Britain. Make a colorful poster telling people why it should not be allowed to die out.

85 It's of less use for people to come to an area from far away and try to save a species, than for local people to get involved. The locals need to have input into the rescue effort. Through ecotourism, visitors can see rare wildlife without damaging it or the habitat and pay money, which is put toward conservation efforts.

◄ Elephant safaris allow paying tourists to get close to rare rhinos without disturbing them too much.

86 Saving one "flagship" or "headline" species from extinction can help to save whole habitats. Such species usually appeal to the public because they are big and powerful, like tigers and mountain gorillas, or cute and fluffy, like giant pandas and golden lion tamarins.

▼ Setting up wildlife parks and nature reserves helps not only the headline species, such as these gorillas, but all the plants and animals living there.

Should we care?

87 **Why should we care if a species goes extinct?** Especially if it is some small bug in a remote forest, or a worm on the seabed. Does it really matter or affect us in any way?

88 **Many people think that all animals and plants have a right to be here on Earth.** We should not destroy nature for little reason. If we let species die out, it shows we do not care for our surroundings and the natural world. These types of reasons are known as moral and ethical arguments.

89 **There are medical reasons for saving species.** Researchers may discover that a particular type of plant or animal is the source of a new wonder drug to cure illness. If it had gone extinct, we would never know this. Other species can be used for medical research into diseases such as cancers.

90 **Scientific reasons to prevent species dying out are also important.** Extinction reduces biodiversity, which is the variety of living things necessary for the balance of nature. The genes in certain animals or plants could be used in GM, genetic modification, perhaps to improve our farm crops and make our farm animals healthier.

91 **There are also traditional and cultural reasons for caring about extinction.** Some endangered species are important to ethnic groups and tribes for their history, ceremonies, myths and special foods. People should not come to an area from afar with new ways of living and cause habitat loss, introduce new animals, plants and diseases and kill off local species.

▲ The Florida panther is an extremely rare subspecies of cougar, or mountain lion. If it dies out, there will still be other cougars elsewhere. So would its disappearance matter?

I DON'T BELIEVE IT!

In the 1800s, European explorers in Australia captured now-extinct creatures including pig-footed bandicoots. But when the explorers got lost and hungry, they ate the bandicoots.

Gone forever?

92 People once thought that extinction is forever, but future science may change this view. The idea of bringing extinct animals or plants back to life can be seen through films such as *Jurassic Park*. Scientists use a species' eggs, its genes or its genetic material such as DNA (de-oxyribonucleic acid).

▲ In the *Jurassic Park* stories, dinosaurs were recreated from their preserved genes and hatched in egg incubators.

93 In 2009, a baby Pyrenean ibex, a subspecies of the goat-like Spanish ibex, was born. Its mother was a goat, but its genes came from one of the last Pyrenean ibexes, which had died out by 2000. The young ibex was a genetic copy. It died after birth, but it showed what might be possible in future.

▼ Why the Pyrenean ibex died out is unclear, but it may have been the result of infectious diseases.

94 To revive extinct species, there are many problems to solve in genetic engineering, altering DNA, cloning and similar methods. However, scientists are taking samples of DNA and other material from all kinds of sources, such as frozen mammoths, dodo bones, the dead seeds of extinct plants, and even long-gone humans, to carry out experiments and see what can be done.

▲ The Barbary lion of North Africa was thought to be extinct from the 1920s, but genetic tests have revealed several living in zoos.

▼ The Quagga Project selects and breeds the most quagga-like zebras over many generations.

95 The quagga, which went extinct in 1883, was a subspecies of the plains zebra of southern Africa. It had zebra stripes on its front half but was plain brown at the rear. The Quagga Project aims to "breed back" quaggas. This is done by choosing plains zebras that look most like quaggas, and allowing them to mate. Gradually, after several generations, the young of plains zebras should look more and more like quaggas.

Looking to the future

96 In the future, living things will continue to go extinct, with or without human meddling —because that is the nature of life and how it evolves. The damage we are doing to the world, especially with habitat loss and climate change, means that the rate of extinction will only increase.

Ardipithecus ramidus
Extinct: 4.5 million years ago

Australopithecus afarensis
Extinct: 3.5 million years ago

Homo ergaster
Extinct: 1.9 million years ago

Homo erectus
Extinct: 1.7 million years ago

97 What about our own kind, human beings? Over the past four million years, there have probably been more than 20 different species of humans and their close cousins on Earth. Only one is left now—ourselves, modern humans, known as *Homo sapiens*. All others have become extinct.

▲ There have been many different species of human throughout history. Despite advances such as stone tools and controlling fire, they all became extinct.

98 A recent human extinction is the Neanderthal people, *Homo neanderthalensis*. They lived about 250,000 years ago across northern Europe and Asia. As modern humans spread from Africa into Europe and Asia, Neanderthals died out. Whether modern people killed them, or were better at finding food and shelter, is not clear.

I DON'T BELIEVE IT!

Recent surveys indicate that 1 in 8 bird species are at risk of extinction, and within 100 years this could rise to 1 in 4. And birds are a lot less threatened than many other animal groups.

99

Surviving even later than the Neanderthals, but still becoming extinct, were the "hobbit people" on the island of Flores, Southeast Asia. Known as *Homo floresiensis*, they were only about 3.3 feet (one meter) tall. They may have survived until less than 15,000 years ago.

▶ The remains of *Homo floresiensis* were discovered in 2003. It may be a new species of extinct human.

Homo floresiensis Extinct: 15,000 years ago

Homo heidelbergensis Extinct: 600,000 years ago

Homo neanderthalensis Extinct: 100,000 years ago

100

In the distant future, will humans become extinct? Our knowledge of the natural world, and the harm we are doing it, suggests that our species will not last forever. But humans have shown great skill at surviving all kinds of problems, and are likely to carry on for a very long time yet.

▶ Can modern humans use their wit and intelligence to survive—while also saving wild species?

Homo sapiens Still alive today

Index